W9-CII-079

Jesko

21st Century Skills Library

HEALTHY FOR LIFE
SURFING

Jim Fitzpatrick

Cherry Lake Publishing
Ann Arbor, Michigan

Published in the United States of America by Cherry Lake Publishing
Ann Arbor, MI
www.cherrylakepublishing.com

Content Adviser: Thomas Sawyer, EdD, Professor of Recreation and Sports Management,
Indiana State University, Terre Haute, Indiana

Photo Credits: Page 4, © Remi Benali/Corbis; page 6, © Bettmann/Corbis; page 11,
© Jeff Flindt/NewSport/Corbis; page 13, © Karl Weatherly/Corbis; page 19, © Robert
Landau/Corbis; page 23, © ASP Tostee/Handout/Reuters/Corbis

Copyright ©2008 by Cherry Lake Publishing
All rights reserved. No part of the book may be reproduced or utilized in any
form or by any means without written permission from the publisher.

Library of Congress Cataloging-in-Publication Data
Fitzpatrick, Jim, 1948–
  Surfing / by Jim Fitzpatrick.
    p. cm.—(Healthy for life)
  Includes bibliographical references and index.
  ISBN-13: 978-1-60279-019-3 (lib. bdg.)   978-1-60279-093-3 (pbk.)
  ISBN-10: 1-60279-019-1 (lib. bdg.)   1-60279-093-0 (pbk.)
  1. Surfing—Juvenile literature. I. Title. II. Series.
  GV840.S8F58 2008
  797.2'3—dc22   2007004466

Cherry Lake Publishing would like to acknowledge the work of
The Partnership for 21st Century Skills.
Please visit www.21stcenturyskills.org *for more information.*

TABLE OF CONTENTS

CHAPTER ONE

SURFING AROUND THE WORLD

Would you like to walk on water? Try surfing!

When you imagine yourself surfing, where do you see it happening? Hawaii? California? While surfing was invented in Hawaii, and many Californians love to surf, now people around the world enjoy the thrill of riding waves. Today, there are great **surf spots** in Japan, Indonesia, India, Africa, Europe, and North and South America. It seems surfing is popular wherever there is a beach, but nowadays surfing isn't limited to oceans. Wave machines have made it possible to create surfing conditions in other bodies of water. So even people who live far from the beach can enjoy the sport developed by royal Hawaiians long ago.

In 1778, English explorer Captain James Cook became the first Westerner to witness the wonder of surfers riding waves in Hawaii. Surfing had been part of the culture of Hawaii's indigenous people for centuries. By the early 20th century, more people were traveling to the Hawaiian islands. A man named George Freeth is credited with introducing surfing to the mainland United States.

Hawaii's Duke Paoa Kahanamoku became surfing's first true ambassador. Kahanamoku won swimming medals in the Olympic Games in 1912, 1920, and 1924. When not competing, he traveled around the world, sharing his joy of the ocean and of everything "water." At his swimming exhibitions, he also demonstrated surfing. This popularized the sport.

Learning & Innovation Skills

Surfing sounds like a fairly simple sport: you climb on a board and ride a wave. But even simple sports have room for change and innovation. The invention of wave machines has helped make surfing more popular, even in regions where people do not have access to an ocean. Today, there are surf spots in Arizona, Minnesota, Switzerland, and even Saudi Arabia. Advancements like this will help ensure that the sport of surfing will thrive for years to come.

Kahanamoku used an old-style solid wood surfboard. It was large and heavy, and required great strength and skill to use. Not everyone could handle such big boards. For a time, this limited the sport's growth. Then

Duke Kahanamoku (right) popularized surfing around the world in the 1920s.

a Minnesotan named Tom Blake developed hollow surfboards, and by the 1950s, people began shaping surfboards from lighter materials like balsa wood.

Surfing's popularity exploded when foam surfboards were developed in the early 1960s. Suddenly, anyone could get a surfboard and take it to the beach. On some days, it looked like that's just what everyone did! These fiberglass-coated, foam-core surfboards were lightweight and inexpensive. They could be made for surfers of all shapes and sizes.

Movies, TV programs, and magazines like *Surfer* and *Surf Guide* helped fuel interest in surfing. By the mid-1960s, surfing was popular on both coasts of the United States and in France, England, Spain, South Africa, Australia, and New Zealand. There were even guidebooks, like the *Surfing Guide to Southern California*, which explained where to find the best surfing beaches. Today, a book like this might point surfers to beaches on Bali, an island in Indonesia. Surfing has truly become a worldwide phenomenon.

Duke Kahanamoku was world renowned for his skills in the water. But he did more than just compete in swimming and surfing events. He also adapted his talents to help people. For a time, he worked as a lifeguard in Newport Beach, California. During a storm, a boat approaching the city harbor sank, spilling nearly 30 men into the ocean. Kahanamoku saw it happen and took the initiative. He grabbed his surfboard and paddled into the rough seas, rescuing eight of the men himself! The Newport police chief called this effort the "most superhuman surfboard rescue act the world has ever seen."

CHAPTER TWO

WHICH BOARD IS FOR YOU?

You need to be a good swimmer before you take up surfing.

Before you try surfing, you need to ask yourself one simple question: am I a strong swimmer? Duke Kahanamoku had to become an excellent swimmer before his family allowed him to venture out into deeper water to surf on the outer reefs of Hawaii's Waikiki Beach.

After all, wherever you choose to surf, you may end up in deep water. As a result, you might have to swim across currents or recover from wipeouts. And you need to be comfortable with swimming back to shore if you lose your board. Don't go out until you're a good enough swimmer. It may truly mean the difference between life and death.

Once you're a strong enough swimmer, it's time to pick your surfboard. Today's surfboards come in all sizes and shapes for the ever-increasing number of people who enjoy surfing. In the early 20th century, all surfboards were **longboards**. These old-style longboards were 12 to 20 feet (3.6 to 6 meters) long and weighed 75 pounds (34 kilograms) or more. By the early 1960s, lightweight foam surfboards had emerged. By the mid-1970s, **shortboards** had developed. These smaller boards, usually 6 to 8 feet (1.8 to 2.4 m), provide greater speed and maneuverability.

Beginners typically work with longboards. These provide more balance and stability, so they are easier

Learning & Innovation Skills

Shortboards were a great innovation in surfing. They enable surfers all over the world to enjoy a level of speed and exhilarating twists and turns that they never thought possible. But riding a shortboard is not easy. Shortboards can be incredibly fast. You have to be quick thinking and flexible, both physically and mentally. You also have to be able to adapt quickly to whatever the waves bring you. Shortboards are a great challenge, but bring fabulous rewards.

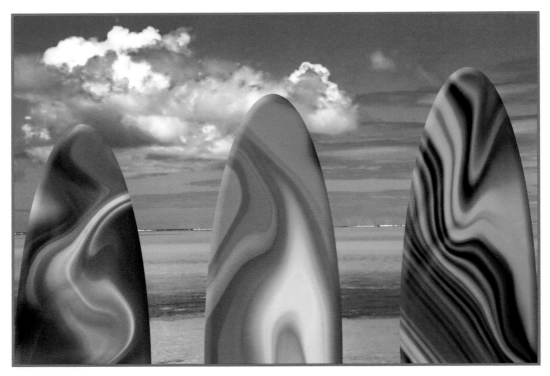

Most surfboards are between 6 and 12 feet (1.8 to 3.6 m) long.

to use when learning. Once beginners have mastered the basics, they can choose to continue using a longboard or make the switch to a shortboard.

Today's modern surfboards are made from a variety of materials, including sophisticated plastics that are virtually indestructible. A few manufacturers also make surfboards with a soft, spongy material on the **deck**, giving surfers added comfort. This is especially useful for beginners who might find themselves falling more often than the experienced surfers.

The type of surfboard a surfer chooses is often determined by the types of waves available. Small waves are easier to ride with a longboard, while it is usually better to ride larger, more powerful waves with a high-performance shortboard, sometimes called a **thruster**. Surfers riding really big waves, like those on the North Shore of Oahu in Hawaii, use special boards called "big

Tube riding—riding inside the curl of a wave— is one of surfing's greatest thrills.

Learning & Innovation Skills

Modern lightweight surfboards have allowed surfers to develop tricks much like those performed by skateboarders and snowboarders. In the early 1960s, the styles, turns, and maneuvers of surfers influenced skateboarders. By the 1980s, surfers began attempting some of the tricks skateboarders were doing. Today, surfers, snowboarders, and skateboarders all seem to be influencing each other!

This collaboration has allowed surfers to find new ways to enjoy their sport. Some longboarders now noseride. In this trick, the surfer stands on the very front of the surfboard. Longboarders and shortboarders can both enjoy tube rides, in which they are actually riding inside the curl of the breaking wave as it moves toward shore. Shortboards are better for getting air—launching into the air above the wave, landing again on the wave's surface, and continuing to ride toward shore. This maneuver is similar to a skateboarder getting air on a ramp. Tricks like this make old-style surfers shake their heads in disbelief!

guns." Big guns are designed specifically to speed along on waves up to 30 feet (9 m) high. Other boards are designed for even larger waves, which are ridden by surfers who are towed into the waves by watercraft.

The size of the surfer and the size of the wave affect the size of the surfboard to use. Ability is also a factor to consider when choosing a board. By matching a surfer's size, ability, and the types of waves available, a surfer can select a board that will provide the best surfing experience. Surfboards usually cost between $150 and $1,000.

CHAPTER THREE

Safe Surfing

Surfing is one of the most exciting and enjoyable sports imaginable. It's an incredible sensation to rush across the surface of the water. But surfing is not without its dangers. Safe surfing is the responsibility of each and every surfer.

A surfer glides across the water.

21st Century Content

Surfing is a relatively safe sport, but injuries do happen. Common surfing injuries include bruises, cuts, sprains, fractures, dislocated shoulders, and stings from marine life. Always bring a first aid kit with you to the beach. This will enable you to treat cuts, bruises, and stings. For more serious injuries, like fractures or a dislocated shoulder, you'll need to see a doctor.

Heat exhaustion and heat stroke are also dangers for surfers. This may seem strange since surfing involves so much water, but surfers sometimes spend hours in the sun on a hot day. Someone who feels dizzy or faint, or has dry or clammy skin, may be suffering from heat exhaustion. The person should be given water to drink and taken out of the sun. In extreme cases, call 911.

The beach itself often has hidden dangers. Surfers frequently seek out beaches that have reefs or rocks underwater because these help create better waves for surfing. Surfers prefer waves that break in one spot and then taper in one direction or another toward shore. Waves breaking over even, sandy bottoms rarely create that type of wave. So, unfortunately, the best surfing beaches usually have underwater hazards. Surfers must pay close attention to where these hazards are, or they may end up with scrapes, bumps, or even broken bones.

Surfers must also keep track of tides and currents, which affect the condition of waves. A rising tide can dramatically increase the size of waves.

To stay safe while surfing, you must pay close attention to the surfers around you. Unlike many sports, surfing has no rule book. Instead, surfers have come up with some unspoken guidelines that are good to keep in mind, especially when surfing with strangers for the first time.

*To stay safe, surfers must know where
there are rocks under the water.*

When you are surfing, you will often encounter other surfers or swimmers on the waves. You and others in the water share a responsibility to stay safe. The safety precautions you take will benefit others. People in the water must communicate effectively with each other. Before going out to the waves, make sure people know where you are and where you will be surfing. That way, they can watch to make sure you are safe. This also helps avoid accidents, because people in the water will know they need to give you the right-of-way as you head toward shore.

Have you ever heard athletes say things like, "Golf is 50 percent mental" or "Keep your head in the game!"? Surfing is also very "mental." It is essential that all surfers keep their heads in the game when they're out in the water. Surfers must also think before they go out. Each surfer is responsible for his or her own safety. Surfers must be familiar with the beach and know the conditions of the tides, currents, and wind.

Once surfers are on the water, they must think fast. They must know what to do if they encounter another surfer or a particular kind of wave. Choosing the right wave also takes concentration. And when you're riding the wave, you make many split-second decisions. Surfing is both mental and physical, a total experience for the mind and body.

The most basic rule among surfers is that the first surfer riding a wave has the right-of-way. When a surfer has caught a wave and is up and riding, no other surfer should take off on the wave in front of the first surfer. Those paddling out must also avoid crossing the path of the surfer on the wave. If everyone in the water follows this basic rule, then everyone will stay safe and get a turn on their own waves.

CHAPTER FOUR

SURFING THE ENVIRONMENT

Surfers spend hours in the ocean in a single day, so it's important to them that the water is not polluted.

Many surfers are deeply concerned about the environment. One reason surfers are so attentive to the environment is that their favorite sport puts them *in* the environment. They want the beaches and ocean where they spend their time to be clean. Many surfers belong to the Surfrider Foundation, a worldwide organization that promotes beach cleanliness

21st Century Content

Because of organizations like the Surfrider Foundation, global awareness of environmental issues and the health of oceans has increased. People all over the world have the responsibility to understand and address global issues like water pollution. That way, they can collaborate to solve these problems. This will ensure that beaches, shorelines, and waters are safe and clean for years to come.

Water from rivers, streams, and storm drains all ends up in the ocean.

and environmental awareness. Its members focus their attention on the health of their local beaches. Surfrider members coordinate water-testing and cleanup activities.

Many famous surf spots, including Malibu and Rincon in Southern California, are at the mouths of creeks. The conditions created at spots where creeks and rivers enter oceans are often ideal for surfers. Surfers at Rincon can sometimes ride for nearly a half mile on waves that begin to break at the creek's mouth and then taper off to one side.

A surfer watches the waves in Malibu, one of the most famous surf spots in the United States.

Don't go in the ocean if a beach is closed. The water might make you sick.

Unfortunately, beaches where creeks enter oceans are often among the most polluted spots along the shore. That's because the water that falls inland collects in those creeks and rivers, and some of that water is polluted. Rain that falls on farmland might carry insecticides or pesticides into the creeks. The creeks then carry these harsh chemicals out to the ocean. Rainwater that has run over streets and parking lots also ends up in the ocean. This water may contain motor oil or litter it has picked up along the way.

Sometimes, beaches must be closed because the water is so polluted. Beach closures typically happen after heavy rainstorms, when rivers and creeks are carrying more water into the ocean. The pollution in the water can endanger surfers. Skin infections, colds, and other illnesses have become all too common for surfers who head out too soon after a storm.

Organizations like the Surfrider Foundation lead the way in getting communities involved in keeping their beaches healthy and open to visitors. Surfrider's Blue Water Task Force provides individuals and groups with water-testing equipment. That way, people can take the initiative to monitor and evaluate creek and ocean water themselves. Another project involves labeling street storm drains with stickers or stencils announcing "The Beach Begins Here," which reminds people that anything going down the drain ends up in the ocean.

Surfrider has also developed a program for schools called Respect the Beach. It includes field trips, videos, and hands-on projects designed to help students better understand the importance of healthy coastal lands. Surfers and others concerned about the environment are collaborating to educate others about the steps they can take to make sure our environment is clean and healthy.

CHAPTER FIVE

SURFING IS GOOD FOR YOU!

Most people surf because it is a lot of fun. Surfing has an added benefit, however: it is really good for you. Surfing is a great way to get exercise. From the moment surfers lift their feet from the land, their bodies are

Surfing is a blast!

*Professional surfer Kelly Slater shows
off his moves at a contest in California.*

For many people, surfing is not so much a "sport" as a way to relax and enjoy the environment. Too often, sports end up being about competition and winning. Many surfers feel that contests and rules and leagues should be left to other sports. To them, surfing is more about the beach lifestyle.

Still, surfing contests are held around the world at both the amateur and professional levels. Contestants are judged based on elements like length of ride and level of difficulty. World-class surfing competitions are held at such famous surf spots as the Pipeline in Hawaii, Superbank in Australia, and Jeffrey's Bay in South Africa.

But whether a person is alone at the beach or competing for prize money, the goal is always the same: to enjoy each and every wave you ride!

working to maintain balance and move into the correct position. Paddling out through the water requires strength and timing. When paddling, surfers use nearly every muscle in their upper body to propel themselves forward.

Paddling through the waves requires good upper body strength.

A surfer must adjust his or her body constantly in order to keep balanced.

While the shoulders and upper back are busy paddling, a surfer's lower body must maintain balance and position on the surfboard. Otherwise, the surfer would slip off the board into the water. Of course, surfboards have no steering wheel, so while paddling, the surfer's

21st Century Content

Nutrition is an important part of fitness. If you eat well, you'll feel stronger and better. To be healthy, your body needs protein, vitamins, minerals, and carbohydrates. Carbohydrates give your body energy, but they're not all equally good for you. Get your carbs from whole grains. They're much better for your body. Fruits and vegetables supply you with vitamins and minerals, while meats, nuts, and dairy products take care of your protein needs. Your body also needs some fat, but you'll get plenty from eating cheese, meat, nuts, and other healthy foods. Limit the amount of sugary foods and drinks you consume. And drink a lot of water, especially when you're out in the sun or your body is working hard.

body is constantly making adjustments to steer a straight line. Surfers use their arms and legs to change direction or turn around. When surfers decide to take off on a wave, they paddle harder in order to catch up to the wave's speed. Then the surfers transfer their weight and balance to their feet, beginning a whole new challenge!

Surfing requires great concentration.

Just standing on a surfboard requires tremendous skill.

Standing on a surfboard atop a wave as it races toward the shore is truly remarkable. Staying upright is a huge challenge for beginning surfers, but this only makes the thrill and sense of accomplishment even greater. You're moving, the surfboard is moving, the wave is moving, and the water is moving. All parts of the surfer's body must work in harmony to

Surfing is good for the body and the spirit.

maintain balance. Surfers use turns to speed up and slow down, while also using their bodies to keep the board headed in the direction they want to go. From the tips of their toes to the tops of their heads, surfers use their entire bodies while on the water. It's exhilarating—and exhausting!

Some people burn as many as 500 calories in one hour of surfing. Just sitting on a surfboard calls for coordination of the arms, legs, feet, and upper body—everything about surfing is exercise. But surfers don't think of it like that. They just think they're having fun.

Learning & Innovation Skills

Surfers have made many innovations as they strive for new and better experiences. Some surfers crave big waves. For them, nothing can top riding a mountain of water and surviving. By the late 1990s, a few brave souls were riding waves no one thought could ever be ridden. One of the spots they surfed is called Jaws. It's on the island of Maui in Hawaii. The waves at Jaws are 40 to 50 feet (12 to 15 m) high! They move so quickly, a surfer on a regular surfboard cannot paddle fast enough to catch them!

Then surfers came up with a creative way to catch these big waves. They decided to try having another person drive a small watercraft like a Jet Ski and tow the surfer into the wave. After catching the wave, the surfer drops the towrope. This is called tow-in surfing. It lets surfers enjoy waves that were impossible to ride years ago.

Now there are surf spots around the world that are famous for their tow-in waves. They include Ilha dos Lobos in Brazil, Teahupoo in Tahiti, and Mavericks in California.

Glossary

deck (DEHK) the part of the board that a surfer stands on

longboards (LAWNG-bordz) big surfboards at least 9 feet (2.7 m) long, which are usually used for relatively small, slow waves

noseride (NOZE-ride) a trick performed on a longboard in which the surfer stands on the very front of the board

shortboards (SHORT-bordz) surfboards, usually 6 to 8 feet (1.8 to 2.4 m) long, that provide good control and are used for big, fast waves

surf spots (SURF SPOTS) beaches where conditions create good surfing waves

thruster (THRUS-tur) a high-performance shortboard

tow-in surfing (TOE-in SURF-ing) a type of surfing in which a surfer holding a towrope is pulled into position by another person riding a small watercraft, allowing the surfer to catch extremely large waves

tube rides (TOOB rydz) maneuvers in which a surfer is riding inside the curl of a breaking wave

FOR MORE INFORMATION

Books

Baker, Tim. *Go Surf*. New York: DK Publishing, 2007.

Bass, Scott. *Surf! Your Guide to Longboarding, Shortboarding, Tubing, Aerials, Hanging Ten, and More*. Washington, DC: National Geographic, 2003.

Voeller, Edward A. *Extreme Surfing*. Mankato, MN: Capstone Press, 2000.

Web Sites

Surfrider Foundation
www.surfrider.org
Learn how you can help promote healthy beaches

Surfline
www.surfline.com
A resource for finding wave conditions at surf spots around the world

Surf Industry Manufacturers Association (SIMA)
www.sima.com
Learn more about new surfing products

INDEX

ABOUT THE AUTHOR

Jim Fitzpatrick has been surfing since his boyhood days in La Jolla, California. A boyhood surfer's dream came true when Jim's family moved to a house on Topanga Beach in Malibu in 1960. "High tides would wash up under our living room!" recalls Jim. An active surfer for more than 50 years, Jim is a past member of the board of directors of the Surf Industry Manufacturers Association, and he still works closely with surf companies around the world. Each summer, Jim runs the Santa Barbara Montessori School's surf camp. At the camp, Jim shares his love of the ocean with children enrolled in the school he and his wife, Frances, founded more than 30 years ago.